Discover the

1

With more than 1.5 million overnight tourists in 2023, Madeira was the fourth most visited region in Portugal. The most important part with a total of 476 million were tourists from Portugal.

On the second place with a number of 335 million overnight tourists were visitors from:

Your Answer

A United Kingdom
B Germany
C Poland

Check your Answer with the Solution at the end of the Book.

Discover the Secrets of... *Madeira*

2

With an area of 740 km^2, Madeira is the largest island in the autonomous region of Madeira.

In addition to the uninhabited archipelago of Ihlas Desartas and Selvagens, the following island belongs to this region:

Your Answer

- A Ponta Delgada
- B Porto Santo
- C Santa Cruz

Check your Answer with the Solution at the end of the Book.

Discover the Secrets of…
Madeira

D. Acker

Copyright © 2024 D. Acker

All information without guarantee.

Dear reader,

the beauty of traveling is the personal enrichment through experiencing other cultures, the experience of alternative ways of life, the joy of discovering new things and learning more about the past of our world. A trip to another country is often also a journey into history and helps to better understand one's own present.

The questions in this book cover a wide range and are intended to increase not only knowledge but, above all, interest in your travel destination. Maybe you read this book long before you start your trip, or maybe you only read it at the airport or during your journey. I hope you enjoy answering the questions in this book and that you remember as many of the facts as possible. Maybe it will even help you enjoy your vacation more consciously.

I would very much appreciate your positive feedback on Amazon and wish you a pleasant and relaxing holiday on Madeira.

★★★★★

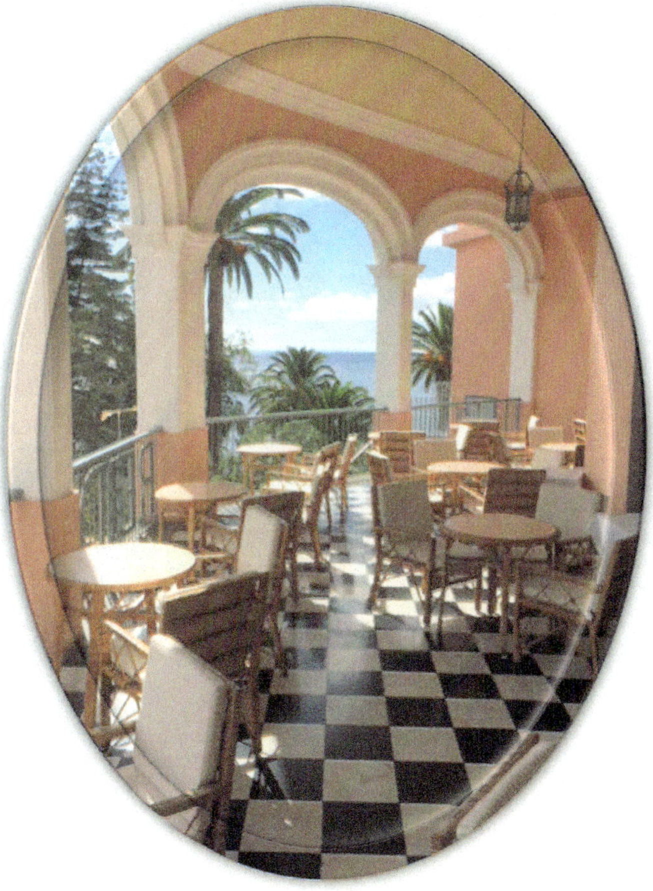

Discover the Secrets of... Madeira

3

Madeira was already listed as an island in the Medici's maritime atlas of 1351. The island was officially taken over by Portugal through the Portuguese João Gonçalves Zarco.

This was in:

Your Answer

A 1419
B 1492
C 1789

Check your Answer with the Solution at the end of the Book.

Discover the Secrets of... Madeira

4

Since 1999, the island has been listed as a UNESCO World Heritage Site due to its Laurissilva Forest, which covered almost the entire island. It is a rare subtropical forest, which occupies today around 15,000 hectares, corresponding to nearly 20% of the island.

The Island also owes its name to this wealth of forests, as Madeira translates as:

Your Answer

- A Flower ☐
- B Forest ☐
- C Wood ☐

Check your Answer with the Solution at the end of the Book.

Discover the Secrets of... Madeira

5

In 1580, Portugal, along with Madeira, fell to the Spanish crown because the Portuguese royal family had no successor. It was only in the middle of the 17th century that Portugal became independent again - with the help of England.

Madeira received its first separate administration, which founded the autonomous republic, in:

Your Answer

A 1964
B 2002
C 1976

Check your Answer with the Solution at the end of the Book.

Discover the Secrets of... Madeira

6

The Airport of Madeira opened in 1964 with a runway of 1.750 yd. Since this runway proved to be too short for larger aircraft, it was expanded in 2000 with a total of 180 pillars, some of which were attached to the seabed.

The runway today measures:

Your Answer

A 2,077.9 yd
B 3,041.3 yd
C 1,947.7 yd

Check your Answer with the Solution at the end of the Book.

Discover the Secrets of... Madeira

7

Madeira is known as the island of eternal spring. The best time to travel is between April and October, as in winter temperatures can drop to 16°C and heavy rainfall can occur.

The average annual temperature is:

Your Answer

A 11°C
B 14°C
C 19°C

Check your Answer with the Solution at the end of the Book.

Discover the Secrets of... Madeira

8

The island's airport was renamed Aeroporto de Cristiano Ronaldo on March 29, 2017. The Portuguese football star was born in Funchal and holds the world record for most international goals.

His Birthday is:

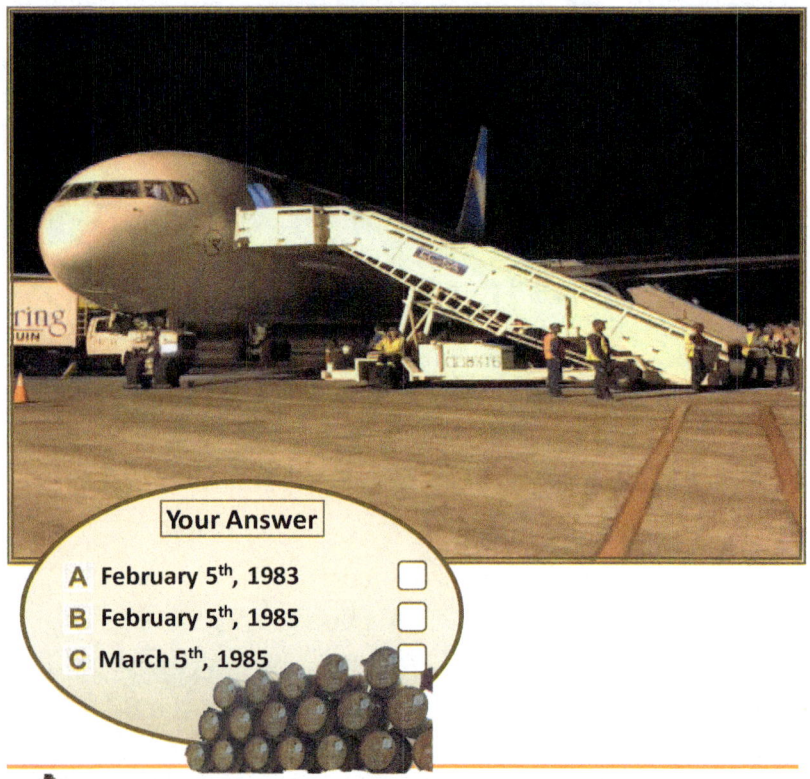

Your Answer

A February 5th, 1983
B February 5th, 1985
C March 5th, 1985

Check your Answer with the Solution at the end of the Book.

Discover the Secrets of... Madeira

9

At over 800 meters above sea level, Ribeiro Frio is one of the island's largest wetlands with extensive laurel forests. 80,000 fish are bred every year in the pools fed by the mountain water of the "cold river".

It is a matter of:

Your Answer

- **A** Trout
- **B** Scabbardfish
- **C** Salmon

Check your Answer with the Solution at the end of the Book.

Discover the Secrets of... *Madeira*

Discover the Secrets of... Madeira

10

Madeira's national flower is the strelitzia. However, this plant, which belongs to the banana family, does not come from Madeira, but was only introduced to the island in the middle of the 19th century.

It originally comes:

Your Answer

A from Southafrica
B from Japan
C from Korea

Check your Answer with the Solution at the end of the Book.

Discover the Secrets of... Madeira

11

As of January 1, 2024, 10,029,198 people lived in Portugal. With more than 500,000 inhabitants, Lisbon is the largest city in the country.

The autonomous region of Madeira had, at the end of 2022, a population of:

Your Answer

A 198,202 people
B 253,259 people
C 407,321 people

Check your Answer with the Solution at the end of the Book.

Discover the Secrets of... Madeira

12

Madeira has ideal conditions for agriculture thanks to its mild climate and nutrient-rich soil.

While cane sugar, grain and wine were previously exported, today the most important agricultural export product is:

Your Answer

A the Banana ☐
B the Pineapple ☐
C the Citron ☐

Check your Answer with the Solution at the end of the Book.

Discover the Secrets of... Madeira

13

Almost 40% of Madeira's entire population lives in the capital Funchal. In 1508 Funchal received city rights for the first time. The name of the city translates as "fennel"

The city coat of arms awarded by King Manuel I shows:

Your Answer

A One Laurel Branch ☐
B Three Gold Crowns ☐
C Five Sugarloaf Montains ☐

Check your Answer with the Solution at the end of the Book.

Discover the Secrets of... Madeira

14

In recent years, Madeira has made significant efforts to protect the climate. Charging e-mobiles is now possible in almost 109 charging stations on the island.

The share of electricity from renewable energies on the island is expected to increase until 2026 to:

Your Answer

A 78%
B 50%
C 30%

Check your Answer with the Solution at the end of the Book.

Discover the Secrets of... Madeira

15

The Austrian Empress, born Elisabeth Amalie Eugenie von Wittelsbach, spent almost half a year in Madeira in 1860/61 to reduce her lung disease. She became famous under the nickname her siblings gave her.

It was:

Your Answer

A Honey
B Sissi
C Sunny

Check your Answer with the Solution at the end of the Book.

Discover the Secrets of... Madeira

🌸 16

With the exception of Prainha, most of Madeira's natural beaches are made of pebbles. In Calheta and Machico, two artificially created lagoons invite you to swim.

The sand for this comes from:

Your Answer

- **A** from Dubai
- **B** from Porto Santo
- **C** from the Sahara

Check your Answer with the Solution at the end of the Book.

Discover the Secrets of... Madeira

17

The tomb of Charles I of Habsburg is located in the Nossa Senhora do Monte.

He died of pneumonia in Monte in 1918 and was the last emperor:

Your Answer

A from Austria
B from Suisse
C from Germany

Check your Answer with the Solution at the end of the Book.

Discover the Secrets of... Madeira

18

The luxury hotel founded by William Reid opened in 1891, three years after his death. It has been called "Belmond Reid's Palace" since 2014 and has belonged to the French LVMH group since 2018. It has 128 rooms and 35 suites, with the "Presidential Suite" being the most beautiful.

One night in this suite costs:

Your Answer

A 2,006 GBP
B 1,430 GBP
C 285 GBP

Check your Answer with the Solution at the end of the Book.

Discover the Secrets of... Madeira

19

The first artificial canals were built as early as the 15th century to direct the water that collects from the rains on the island's mountains in the north to the southern part of the island.

Regulate the water supply to the individual fields is done by:

Your Answer

A Aquateiros ☐
B Lavadros ☐
C Lavadeiros ☐

Check your Answer with the Solution at the end of the Book.

Discover the Secrets of... Madeira

20

The "Belmond Reid's Palace" is located on a rocky headland above Funchal in the middle of a subtropical garden. In the years from 1950, a famous British minister was often a guest at this hotel and relaxed on the island while painting.

His name was:

Your Answer

A Winston Churchill
B Stanley Baldwin
C Harald Wilson

Check your Answer with the Solution at the end of the Book.

Discover the Secrets of... Madeira

21

The Jardim Bontânico da Madeira is located on the former Reid family estate northeast of Funchal. The family's former mansion has housed a natural history museum with various animal specimens since 1982.

What species of mammal was hunted from Caniçal until 1981?

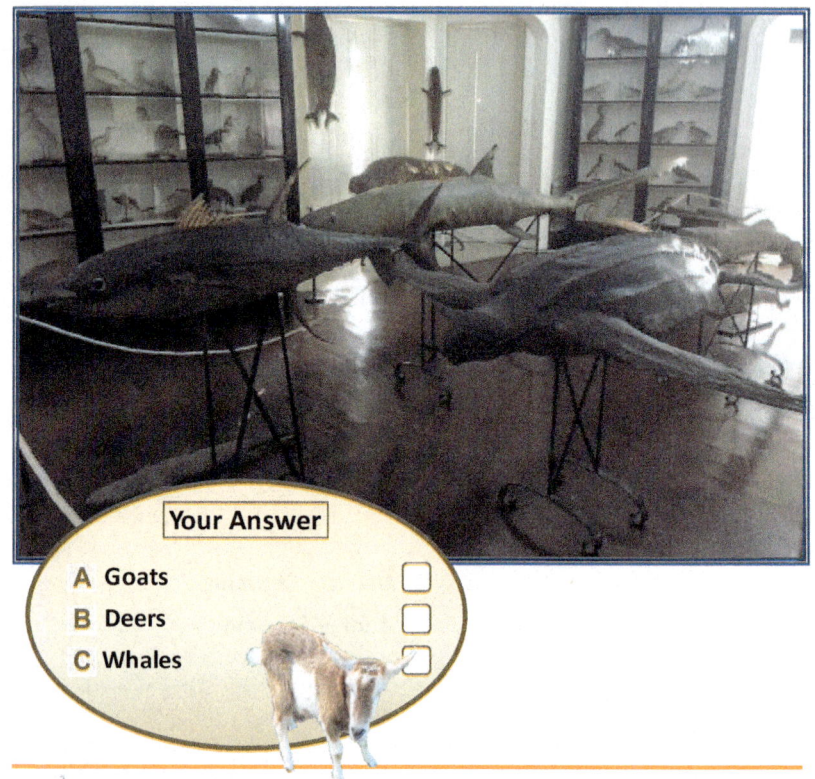

Your Answer

A Goats
B Deers
C Whales

Check your Answer with the Solution at the end of the Book.

Discover the Secrets of... Madeira

22

The corona pandemic created new working conditions through home working. Madeira therefore launched a program in December 2020 to enable foreign workers to telework on the island for one to a maximum of six months.

Since the beginning of the project, Madeira and Porto Santa counted from these Digital Nomads over:

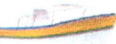

Your Answer

A 11,200
B 8,450
C 4,280

Check your Answer with the Solution at the end of the Book.

Discover the Secrets of... Madeira

23

Only 50 km northeast of Madeira is the island of Porto Santo with its extensive sandy beach. The small windmill near Camacha is a popular excursion destination.

Which famous sailor came to Madeira as a sugar trader and married the daughter of the legate captain Perestrelo on the island of Porto Santo?

Your Answer

A Christoph Columbus ☐
B Francis Drake ☐
C John Hawkins ☐

Check your Answer with the Solution at the end of the Book.

Discover the Secrets of... *Madeira*

Discover the Secrets of... Madeira

24

As an island of volcanic origin, Madeira is very mountainous. With the Cabo Girão, which drops over 634 yd, the island has the second highest cliff in the world.

Its highest mountain, Pico Ruivo, measures:

Your Answer

A 2,299 yd
B 1,471 yd
C 2,036 yd

Check your Answer with the Solution at the end of the Book.

Discover the Secrets of... Madeira

25

Agriculture on its current scale would not be possible without the famous irrigation canals, the levadas, on Madeira. The paths created by workers during canal construction and maintenance are now widely used hiking trails.

They have a total length of:

Your Answer

A 715 miles
B 1,336 miles
C 1,087 miles

Ribeiro Bonito
2,4 Km

PR 18

Check your Answer with the Solution at the end of the Book.

Discover the Secrets of... Madeira

26

The beef skewer, usually seasoned with lots of garlic, is a specialty of the island. In the past, the pieces of meat were grilled on bay leaf skewers, but today cast iron skewers are mostly used.

This specialty is called:

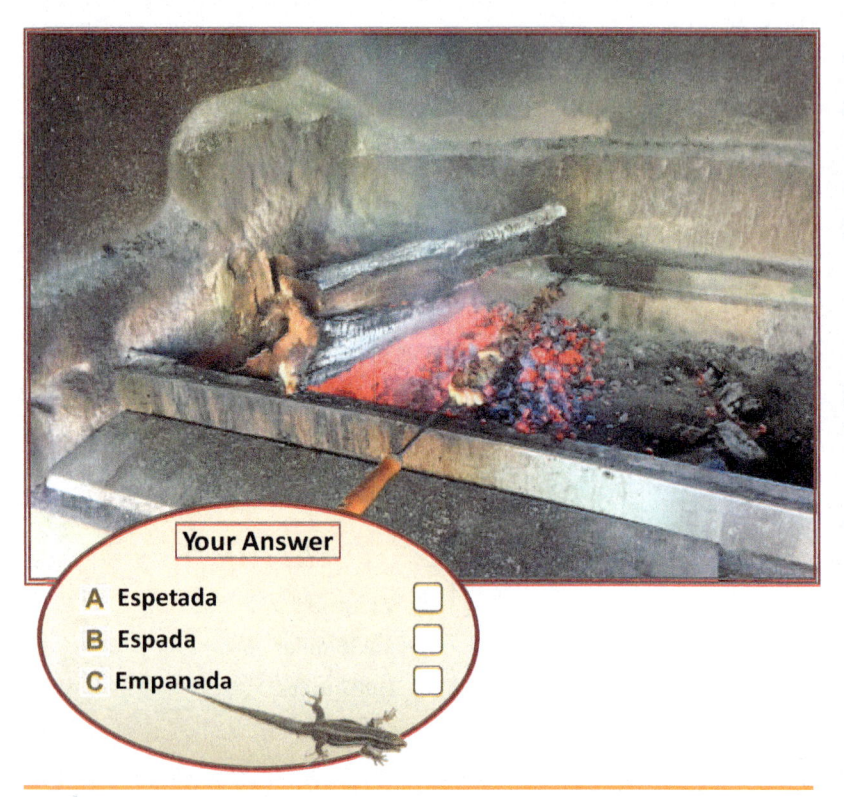

Your Answer

A Espetada
B Espada
C Empanada

Check your Answer with the Solution at the end of the Book.

Discover the Secrets of... Madeira

27

Due to its location, Madeira offers a large selection of fish dishes and seafood. In addition to the bacalhau, the stockfish popular throughout Portugal, the black scabbardfish is a particular specialty of the island.

It is often served with bananas and is called:

Your Answer

A Caldeirada de peixe
B Espetada preta
C Espada preta

Check your Answer with the Solution at the end of the Book.

Discover the Secrets of... Madeira

28

Madeira is not a wine that is drunk in large quantities, but is **often served** as an aperitif or as a dessert wine. It can be **classified** into three varieties, Sercial, Boal and Malvasia.

The sercial is the:

Your Answer

A most dry
B sweetest
C most acidic

Check your Answer with the Solution at the end of the Book.

Discover the Secrets of... Madeira

29

According to legend, Christopher Columbus was confirmed in his suspicion that there must be land on the other side of the Atlantic when he accidentally found a piece of fruit on the beach. Because this fruit did not exist on Madeira or Porto Santo.

It was a:

Your Answer

A Pear
B Cucumber
C Bean

Check your Answer with the Solution at the end of the Book.

Discover the Secrets of... Madeira

30

A hike through the Caldeirão Verde is one of the most popular and spectacular levada hikes on the island, because in many places the levada is carved into the rock face.

Continuing along the path from Caldeirão Verde, you will reach:

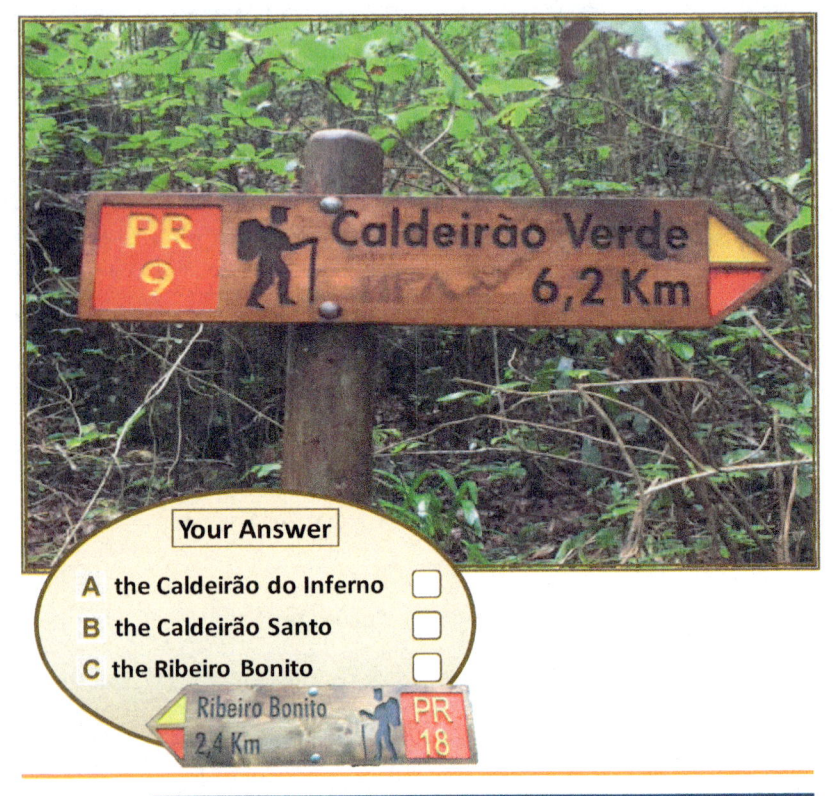

Your Answer

A the Caldeirão do Inferno ☐
B the Caldeirão Santo ☐
C the Ribeiro Bonito ☐

Check your Answer with the Solution at the end of the Book.

Discover the Secrets of... Madeira

31

On the north coast of Madeira, the 590 meter high Penha de Águia, the Eagle Rock, is an elevation that can be seen from far away.

He owes his name to:

Your Answer

A formerly resident ospreys ☐
B The shape of the rock ☐
C The difficulty of accessibility ☐

Check your Answer with the Solution at the end of the Book.

Discover the Secrets of... Madeira

32

In the historic old town of Funchal is the Mercado dos Lavradores, designed by Edmundo Tavares and inaugurated in 1940. The beautiful market hall is divided into three large areas.

You can comfortably drink an espresso in the cafés in the area, which is called in Portuguese:

Your Answer

A Café con leche
B Mokka
C Bica

Check your Answer with the Solution at the end of the Book.

Discover the Secrets of... Madeira

33

Since the waterfront promenade was completed in 2011, it has been easy to walk from Funchal's hotel district to Camara de Lobos. Camara de Lobos is one of the oldest fishing villages in Madeira. The harbor with its colorful fishing boats is a popular destination for tourists.

His name means:

Your Answer

A Monk Seal Cave
B Old Port
C Lobster Coast

Check your Answer with the Solution at the end of the Book.

Discover the Secrets of... Madeira

34

Some farmers on Madeira still live from growing sugar cane, which was already grown on the island in the 15th century and brought wealth to the island in the age of "white gold". The Aguardente de Cana de Açúcar is now used in a drink whose designation of origin has been protected in Madeira since March 2014.

It is called:

Your Answer

A Madeira libre
B Poncha
C Pancho

Check your Answer with the Solution at the end of the Book.

Discover the Secrets of... Madeira

35

In the 15th century, a bread became widespread on the island that, due to its flat shape, could be baked on basalt plates instead of in ovens. Since bread making was reserved for the nobility and was subject to a high tax, it was called cake.

The Portuguese name is:

Your Answer

A Bolo do caco
B Pastéis de nata
C Bolo de Belem

Check your Answer with the Solution at the end of the Book.

Discover the Secrets of... Madeira

36

As early as the 19th century, the wealthy merchants based in Monte used basket sleighs as a kind of transport to be driven to their offices in Funchal. This ride is now very popular, especially among tourists.

The sleigh drivers are called:

Your Answer

A **Empregados**
B **Montenos**
C **Carreiros**

Check your Answer with the Solution at the end of the Book.

Discover the Secrets of... *Madeira*

Discover the Secrets of... Madeira

37

The fruit called fruta da Costela-de-adão or Monstera deliciosa can be found at many weekly markets in Madeira.

Its English name is:

Your Answer

A Austria cheese plant
B Swiss cheese plant
C Green Plant

Check your Answer with the Solution at the end of the Book.

Discover the Secrets of... Madeira

38

The village of Santana takes its name from the small chapel of Santa Ana, built in the 16th century. A church was built in its place in the 17th century. The small village on the north coast became famous for its thatched houses (Casas de Colmo), which are now listed as historical monuments.

How many of these houses still exist in Santana and São Jorge:

Your Answer

A 10 Original houses
B 100 Original houses
C 1,000 Original houses

Check your Answer with the Solution at the end of the Book.

Discover the Secrets of... Madeira

39

A picturesque village is Prazeres with its chapel Nossa Senhora dos Prazeres. Next to the church is the Quinta Pedagógica with its herb garden, small tea house and zoo. The villa-like houses of the wealthy class used to be called quintas.

The term "quinta-feira" means:

Your Answer

A Large house ☐
B Small farm ☐
C Thursday ☐

Check your Answer with the Solution at the end of the Book.

Discover the Secrets of... Madeira

40

The viewpoint at Cabo Girão is a popular meeting point for tourists to enjoy the sunset. With its glass viewing platform, the viewing point offers a special experience. In addition, numerous viewing points on Madeira offer unique panoramas.

They are pointed out with the sign:

Your Answer

A **Point de vue**
B **Belvédère**
C **Miradouro**

Check your Answer with the Solution at the end of the Book.

Discover the Secrets of... Madeira

41

The melancholic musical style of Fado, which is inextricably linked to Portuguese culture, is often referred to as the "longing of the heart".

The name Fado is derived from the Latin word "fatum" and means:

Your Answer

A Fate, destiny
B Eternity
C Grief, sorrow

Check your Answer with the Solution at the end of the Book.

Discover the Secrets of... Madeira

42

There are around 760 wild plant species in Madeira. Many species were imported and only became native to the island over the years. Species that are unique and do not occur anywhere else in the world are called endemic.

The total of endemic plants in Madeira is approximately:

Your Answer

A 440 endemic plants
B 240 endemic plants
C 140 endemic plants

Check your Answer with the Solution at the end of the Book.

Discover the Secrets of... Madeira

43

The Portuguese explorers landed in the natural harbor of Machico in 1419 and in the early years the city functioned as the capital. Every year, the residents of the town celebrate the wooden crucifix, which was miraculously found after the flood in 1803, with a festival.

The festival takes place:

Your Answer

A October 3
B October 8 & 9
C 4th of July

Check your Answer with the Solution at the end of the Book.

Discover the Secrets of... Madeira

44

In 1566, fleeing from pirates, nuns of the Order of Santa Clara sought shelter in a valley that can only be reached via rocky paths. These paths are still well preserved today and make the "Valley of the Nuns" a popular excursion destination.

His name is:

Your Answer

A Boca da Corida
B Curral das Freiras
C Colmeal

Check your Answer with the Solution at the end of the Book.

Discover the Secrets of... Madeira

45

Rabaçal is a popular hiking region on Madeira, to which day tours are also offered from Funchal. The region is located on the western edge of the Paúl da Serra plateau.

In Portuguese "Paúl" means:

Your Answer

- **A** Large Field
- **B** Desert
- **C** Swamp

Check your Answer with the Solution at the end of the Book.

Discover the Secrets of... Madeira

46

In various places, sea swimming pools make it possible to swim in the Atlantic, which is otherwise difficult to do due to the lack of natural beaches. When there are strong waves, swimming in these swimming pools is not entirely safe.

The most beautiful sea swimming pool on the island is located in:

Your Answer

A Santa Cruz
B Jardim do Mar
C Porto Moniz

Check your Answer with the Solution at the end of the Book.

Discover the Secrets of... Madeira

47

The 15th-century Matriz de São Bento church is considered the most visited church on the island. It is located in the fishing village of Ribeira Brava on the southwest coast of the island, which owes its name to a small torrent.

Because Ribeira Brava means translated:

Your Answer

- **A** Wild River ☐
- **B** Calm River ☐
- **C** Small River ☐

Check your Answer with the Solution at the end of the Book.

Discover the Secrets of... Madeira

48

The cabins of the Teleféricos da Madeira are visible from far away in Funchal. The most famous routes are the Cable Car from Funchal to Monte and the Cable Car that leads from Monte to the Botanical Garden.

The total number of these Cable Cars in Madeira today is:

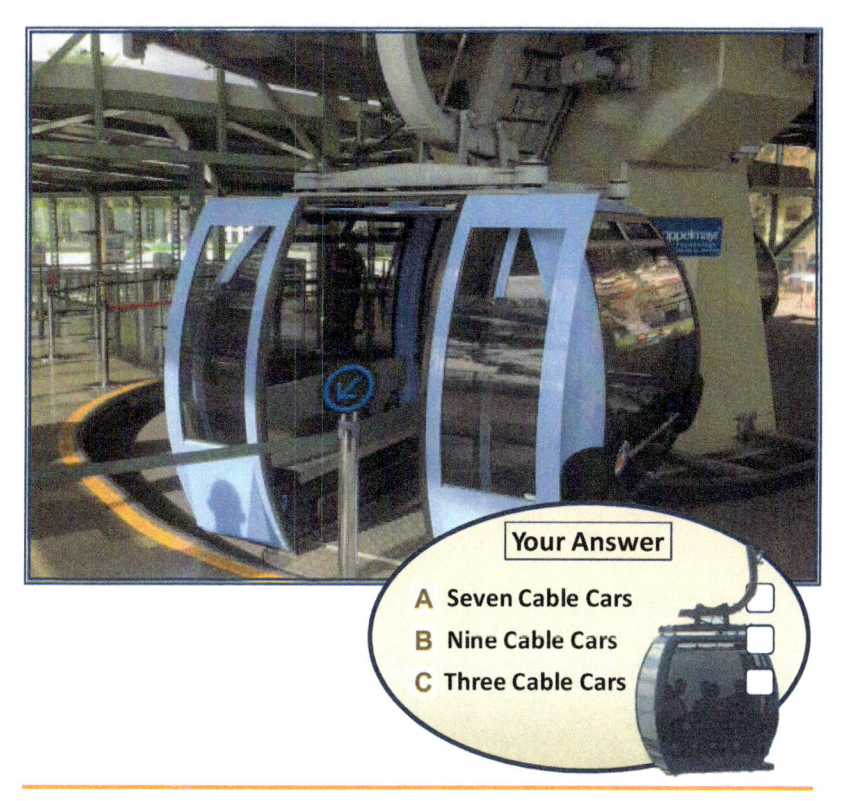

Your Answer

A Seven Cable Cars
B Nine Cable Cars
C Three Cable Cars

Check your Answer with the Solution at the end of the Book.

Discover the Secrets of... Madeira

49

Madeira is located above the African plate and was formed by volcanic activity in several phases. The lava caves of Sao Vincente are the first caves opened to the public in Portugal in October 1996. Due to an earthquake, the caves have been temporarily closed in 2018.

The caves of Sao Vincente were created:

Your Answer

A around 340.000 years ago ☐
B around 510.000 years ago ☐
C around 890.000 years ago ☐

Check your Answer with the Solution at the end of the Book.

Discover the Secrets of… *Madeira*

Discover the Secrets of... Madeira

🌿 50

At nearly 6,000 feet, the Pico do Arieiro is the third-highest peak on the island. The hike from this mountain to the Pico Ruivo is the most famous on the island, but with a lot of steps also very challenging.

The total distance of this hike is:

Your Answer

A 7,5 Miles
B 3,2 Miles
C 14,2 Miles

Check your Answer with the Solution at the end of the Book.

SOLUTIONS

Discover the Secrets of... Madeira

Question		Correct Answer	Question Level	Points	Your Points Reader A	Reader B
1	A	United Kingdom		2		
2	B	Porto Santo		1		
3	A	in 1419		3		
4	C	Wood		1		
5	C	1976		2		
6	B	3,041.3 yd		3		
7	C	19°C		1		
8	B	February 8th, 1985		2		
9	A	Trout		2		
10	A	from Southafrica		2		
11	B	253,259		3		
12	A	the Banana		1		
13	C	Five Sugarloaf Montains		2		
14	B	50,0%		3		
15	B	Sissi		1		
16	C	from the Sahara		2		
17	A	from Austria		2		
Subtotal				33		

Discover the Secrets of... *Madeira*

Discover the Secrets of... Madeira

Question		Correct Answer	Question Level	Points	Your Points Reader A	Reader B
			Subtotal from page 1	33		
18	A	2,006 GBP	🚦	2		
19	C	Lavadeiros	🚦	2		
20	A	Winston Churchill	🚦	1		
21	C	Whales	🚦	1		
22	A	11,200	🚦	3		
23	A	Cristoph Kolumbus	🚦	1		
24	C	2,036 yd	🚦	3		
25	B	1,336 miles	🚦	3		
26	A	Espetada	🚦	2		
27	C	Espada preta	🚦	2		
28	A	most dry	🚦	2		
29	C	Bean	🚦	3		
30	A	the Caldeirão do Inferno	🚦	2		
31	A	formerly resident ospreys	🚦	3		
32	C	Bica	🚦	1		
33	A	Monk Seal Cave	🚦	2		
34	B	Poncha	🚦	1		
Subtotal				67		

Discover the Secrets of... Madeira

Question	Correct Answer	Question Level	Points	Your Points Reader A	Your Points Reader B
		Subtotal from page 2	67		
35 A	Bolo do caco		1		
36 C	Carreiros		2		
37 A	Austria cheese plant		2		
38 B	100 Original houses		2		
39 C	Thursday		2		
40 C	Miradouro		1		
41 A	Fate, destiny		1		
42 C	140 endemic plants		3		
43 B	October 8 & 9		3		
44 B	Curral das Freiras		2		
45 C	Swamp		2		
46 C	Porto Moniz		3		
47 A	Wild River		2		
48 A	Seven Cable Cars		3		
49 C	around 890.000 years ago		2		
50 A	7,5 Miles		2		
Total			100		

Discover the Secrets of... *Madeira*

Discover the Secrets of... Madeira

Printed in Great Britain
by Amazon